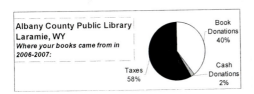

CARTOON NATION presents

EST. 1776

CITIZENSHIP

by Jason Skog
illustrated by Kelly Brown

———◆———

CONSULTANT:
Michael Bailey
Colonel William J. Walsh Associate Professor
of American Government
Georgetown University, Washington, D.C.

Capstone
press

Mankato, Minnesota

Graphic Library is published by Capstone Press,
151 Good Counsel Drive, P.O. Box 669, Mankato, Minnesota 56002.
www.capstonepress.com

1 2 3 4 5 6 13 12 11 10 09 08

Library of Congress Cataloging-in-Publication Data
Skog, Jason.
    Citizenship / by Jason Skog; illustrated by Kelly Brown.
    p. cm. — (Graphic library. Cartoon nation)
    Includes bibliographical references and index.
    ISBN-13: 978-1-4296-1331-6 (hardcover)
    ISBN-10: 1-4296-1331-9 (hardcover)
    ISBN-13: 978-1-4296-1779-6 (softcover pbk.)
    ISBN-10: 1-4296-1779-9 (softcover pbk.)
    1. Citizenship — United States — Juvenile literature. 2. United States — Politics and
government — Juvenile literature. I. Title. II. Series.
JK1759.S617 2008
323.60973 — dc22   2007027336

Summary: In political cartoon format, explains the history of United States citizenship, the
    ways people become U.S. citizens, and the responsibilities of U.S. citizens in society.

Art Director and Designer
Bob Lentz

Editor
Christopher L. Harbo

Editor's note: Direct quotations from primary sources are indicated by a yellow background.

Direct quotations appear on the following pages:
Page 15, from the Oath of Allegiance for Naturalized Citizens, as documented by the U.S.
    Citizenship and Immigration Services (http://www.uscis.gov).
Page 20, from John F. Kennedy's inaugural address on January 20, 1961, as documented at
    the John F. Kennedy Presidential Library and Museum in Boston, Massachusetts
    (http://www.jfklibrary.org).
Page 27, Abraham Lincoln's Gettysburg Address on November 19, 1863, as documented by
    the Library of Congress (http://www.loc.gov/exhibits/gadd/gadrft.html).

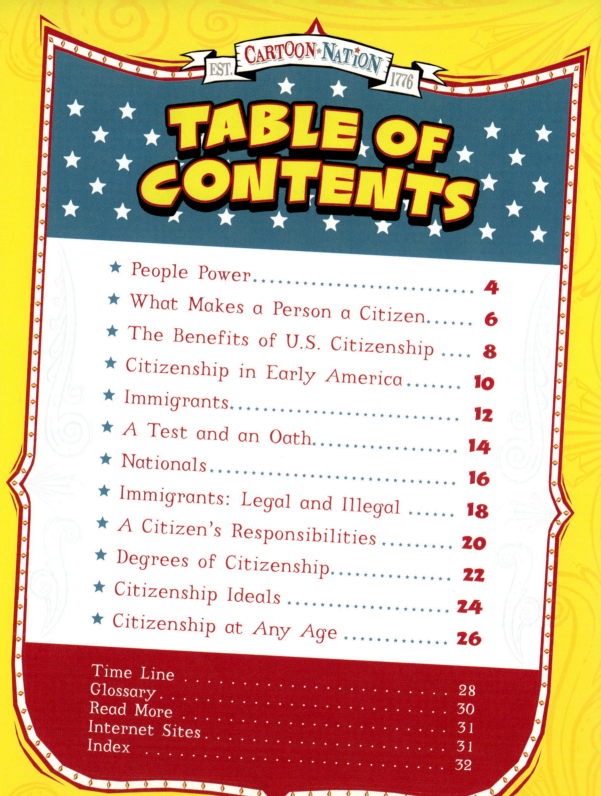

TABLE OF CONTENTS

EST. 1776 · CARTOON NATION

The president of the United States gets to live in the White House, make big decisions, meet important people, and be on television. Yet the power to vote for the president rests with ordinary citizens.

U.S. citizens have more power than you might think. But what is a citizen? A citizen is a legal resident of a country with certain rights and protections. For instance, when U.S. citizens turn 18, they can vote in elections and run for public office.

It may not always seem like it, but citizens make America work. They choose city council members, senators and representatives, and judges and sheriffs. They make the most of their role when they vote, stay informed on issues, and speak out against unfairness.

While the role of a citizen has changed over the years, one thing has remained constant. The power to choose America's leaders and chart the nation's future rests with the people — with the many instead of the few.

VOTING RIGHTS

Not all U.S. citizens have been able to vote after their 18th birthdays. Before the 26th Amendment was approved in 1971, citizens had to be at least 21 to vote. African American men of any age could not vote until 1870, with the passage of the 15th Amendment. And women of all races waited for the 19th Amendment to be passed in 1920 before they could vote.

For most people, becoming an American citizen is as easy as being born in America. That's right! Everybody born in America is automatically a citizen of the United States. Even children born to **illegal immigrants** are citizens if they're born in the United States.

He's adorable.

And he's already an American citizen.

Having American parents also earns a newborn U.S. citizenship. Children born in China, France, or any other country are American citizens if one or both of their parents is a U.S. citizen.

Watch where you stick that pin.

illegal immigrant — a foreign-born person living in a country without legal permission

For those not born in America or to American parents, there are several ways to become a U.S. citizen. In fact, millions of people have become Americans long after they were born in other countries.

CLERK OF THE MONTH

Aren't you a little old to become a citizen, sir?

Old?! You're never too old!

To become citizens, noncitizens go through a process called naturalization.

Step right up folks and become U.S. citizens!

Actually, they learn about the nation's laws and the expectations of citizens. Finally, they must pass a test and take an oath promising to support their country, follow its laws, and be good citizens.

DUAL CITIZENSHIP

Some U.S. citizens are also citizens of other countries. As dual citizens, they can vote in both countries. They also have all the rights and protections provided by both countries.

The Benefits of U.S. Citizenship

Being a citizen of the United States comes with guaranteed protection under the U.S. **Constitution**. U.S. citizens have more freedoms, rights, and opportunities than people in most other countries around the world.

It sure feels safe behind here.

Not bad for a 200-year-old piece of paper!

constitution — the system of laws that state the rights of the people and the powers of the government

As the supreme law of the land, the Constitution provides the freedom to say what you want and practice any religion you choose. You can also speak out against the government.

When In Rome

Your rights as a citizen in America aren't the same when traveling to other countries. You must follow the laws and rules of the country you are visiting. As the saying goes, "When in Rome, do as the Romans do."

Citizenship has more benefits than you might realize. For instance, the government can't search your house or car without a good reason. And citizens have a right to a fair trial in front of a jury made up of other citizens just like yourself.

Who are these clowns?

It's a jury of his peers.

But perhaps most importantly, U.S. citizens enjoy a sense of belonging to a country and the sense of security it provides.

CITIZENSHIP AND THE PRESIDENCY

To be president of the United States, a person must be born a citizen of this country. However, some candidates might someday challenge that law.

California Governor Arnold Schwarzenegger was born an Austrian citizen in 1947.

He became a U.S. citizen after moving to the United States. At this time, he's not allowed to become president. But in America, anything can happen if the Constitution changes.

When the Founding Fathers formed the U.S. government, they wrote the Constitution and later the **Bill of Rights**. The Constitution set up a new government that relied heavily on the involvement of citizens. The Bill of Rights spelled out the freedoms for each citizen.

Please spell "freedom of speech."

SPELLING BEE

That's easy. F-R-E-E . . .

Bill of Rights — the first 10 amendments to the U.S. Constitution

But these documents weren't perfect. Native Americans, slaves, and women didn't share the same rights in the late 1700s. In fact, only rich, white men who owned land could vote or hold elected office.

Our government and laws will be the envy of the world!

U.S. Constitution

And anyone who isn't a wealthy, white man.

Citizens did have enough power in this new country to start change. By the mid-1800s, people wanted elected officials who represented their needs and concerns.

Come on everybody. Let's get out the vote for the Democrats!

The elephant never forgets! Cast your ballot for the Republicans!

Citizens found common ground on issues and began forming political parties. These parties became powerful groups, selecting and supporting candidates for office.

Citizens themselves began getting more involved in the political process. They fought for equal rights, organized political rallies, and wrote letters to their newspapers. Eventually, amendments were added to the Constitution so that all citizens, regardless of race or gender, shared the same rights.

Don't forget a woman's right to vote.

It's right here in the 19th Amendment.

Stop pushing. There's room for all of us in here.

The freedoms and rights of U.S. citizens did not go unnoticed around the world. Soon, millions of people from other countries flocked to America. Some were fleeing poverty or war. Others just wanted to join their families who were already here.

The United States quickly became a "melting pot" of people from other countries. In fact, almost all American citizens have come from some other country or have a family member who did. Along with their suitcases, they brought different personalities, languages, foods, cultures, and religions.

Come on in! The water's GREAT!

And they're still coming! From 2000 to 2005, more than 7.9 million people immigrated to the United States. People come to America to find freedom and opportunities they don't have in their homelands.

ELLIS ISLAND

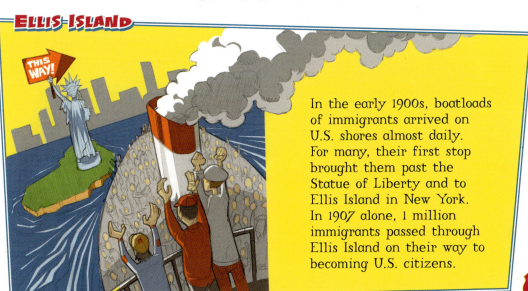

In the early 1900s, boatloads of immigrants arrived on U.S. shores almost daily. For many, their first stop brought them past the Statue of Liberty and to Ellis Island in New York. In 1907 alone, 1 million immigrants passed through Ellis Island on their way to becoming U.S. citizens.

A Test and an Oath

Sharpen your No. 2 pencils and bone up on your U.S. history. It's time to get naturalized!

I thought I was done studying when I finished school.

Becoming a naturalized U.S. citizen requires a few steps. First, immigrants must live in the United States as legal, permanent residents for at least 30 months over five years. They must also be able to speak and write in English. Then they must pass a test.

The test has questions about the colors of the U.S. flag, the branches of government, and the major political parties. It also asks questions about American history and the rights guaranteed under the Constitution.

What do we call the first 10 amendments to the Constitution?

To become president of the United States, what must the person be at birth?

Answer: The Bill of Rights

Answer: A U.S. citizen

If immigrants get at least 60 percent of the questions correct, they take an oath.

An oaf? Isn't that like a big, ugly ogre?

Not an "oaf." An "oath." It's a very serious promise.

. . . I will support and defend the Constitution and laws of the United States of America against all enemies, foreign and domestic . . .

When immigrants pledge the citizenship oath, they promise to be loyal to the U.S. Constitution. They also give up any loyalty to their home countries and promise to defend the United States.

TIGHTER SECURITY

Rules for people coming to the United States have tightened greatly since the terrorist attacks of September 11, 2001. Today, there are many more security concerns. The United States has increased security along the Canadian and Mexican borders where people try to enter into the country.

For most people, being a citizen is pretty straightforward. Either you were born a U.S. citizen or you became one by passing a test and taking an oath. But people living in one of the United States' **territories** have a special status.

USA! USA! USA!

PUERTO RICO! PUERTO RICO!

territory — land under control of a country

U.S. CONSTITUTION

PUERTO RICO

GUAM

The United States controls several territories in other parts of the world. People living in these territories have strong ties with the United States. These territories include the U.S. Virgin Islands, Guam, Puerto Rico, and the Northern Mariana Islands.

Living in a U.S. territory sure has its perks.

Yeah — sand, sun, and so many protections under the U.S. Constitution.

People living in these territories are considered "nationals" of the United States. They are protected by most constitutional laws, but they must also follow the laws of their territories.

Take Puerto Rico, for example. There, native citizens are considered U.S. citizens. They can visit and live in the United States as they please. However, they must be a permanent resident of the United States to vote in U.S. elections. While they're in Puerto Rico, they must follow Puerto Rico's laws and legal systems.

IMMIGRANTS: LEGAL AND ILLEGAL

More than 300 million people live in the United States, but not all of them are here legally. Millions of people have crossed U.S. borders to live and work without permission from the government.

These immigrants are sometimes called "illegal aliens." But they really aren't from outer space.

To enter the United States legally, people from other countries must have permission from the U.S. government. Sometimes a work visa allows them to live and work in America for a certain amount of time. But some people stay longer than they are allowed.

By the looks of it, your work visa expired last week. You'll have to return to your homeland.

Rats!

visa — a document giving a person permission to enter a foreign country

ASYLUM SEEKERS

Some people who try to come to the United States are seeking a place of protection — called asylum — away from their own countries. Sometimes their countries are in a war or they risk being put in jail for their beliefs. The United States government can offer these people protection in this country.

Others try to slip into the country illegally. Often, they are people who left their home countries in search of better lives.

Illegal immigrants face many challenges in the United States, including discrimination, arrest, or **deportation**. Because they are in America illegally, they don't have the same protections and rights as U.S. citizens.

deportation — the act of sending illegal immigrants back to their own countries

In 1961, President John F. Kennedy said:

And so, my fellow Americans: ask not what your country can do for you — ask what you can do for your country.

He had a good point. Citizenship gives you a lot of rights, but it also requires some responsibilities. The country needs citizens to stay informed on issues, obey the laws, serve on juries in court trials, and pay taxes. Citizens have also been called upon to serve the country in times of war.

Citizens who don't follow the laws risk being fined or put in jail. Dodging taxes or jury duty are both crimes.

But I don't want to pay taxes! And I'm too busy for jury duty.

JURY

You're a citizen. You should have thought about that before you were born here.

Citizens who don't participate could be left out of important decisions that affect their lives. If they oppose something planned for their neighborhood, it's up to them to speak up or take action.

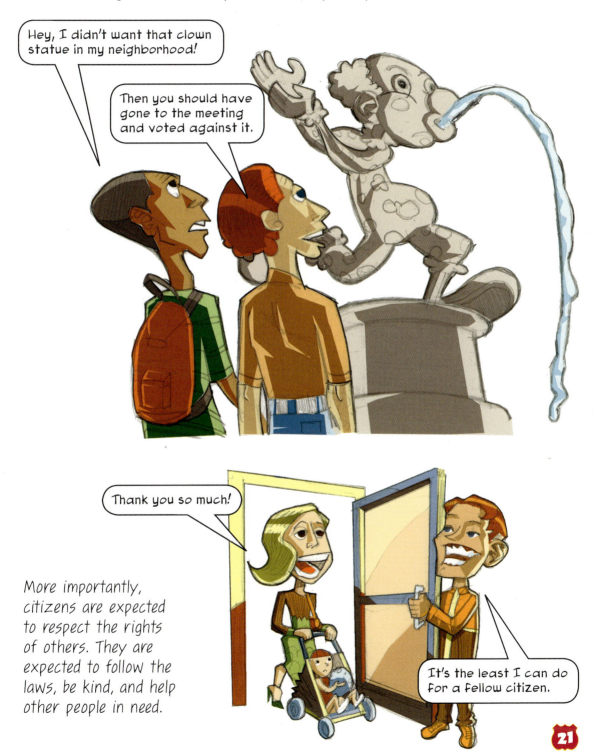

Hey, I didn't want that clown statue in my neighborhood!

Then you should have gone to the meeting and voted against it.

Thank you so much!

More importantly, citizens are expected to respect the rights of others. They are expected to follow the laws, be kind, and help other people in need.

It's the least I can do for a fellow citizen.

DEGREES OF CITIZENSHIP

Citizenship is rarely an all or nothing situation. At one end, some citizens are merely residents of the country. They're like robots. They never vote or get involved in their communities. They have no interest in making their voices heard.

Beep, boop. Politics. Issues. Concerns. Does not compute.

At the other end are people who always vote and take an active interest in a variety of issues. They might organize political rallies or campaigns to make their point. Some people even seek political office, one of the highest levels of citizenship.

I ROCKED THE VOTE!

Come on everybody! Let's get active. Exercise your rights!

Wow. Now that's what I call a citizen.

But most citizens fall somewhere in the middle. They do their best to stay informed on issues. They vote regularly and get involved when an issue affects them.

OBEYING TOO MUCH

In some countries, citizens follow the rules and laws without question. While it may seem like a good situation, it can have bad consequences. Sometimes countries have unfair or harsh laws. The people living there become too afraid to speak or act out against them. For example, in the 1930s and 1940s, Adolph Hitler led Nazi Germany. Many citizens obeyed him without question. This blind obedience allowed Germany to take over much of Europe and kill millions of Jewish people. It was an extreme example of citizens who were loyal without question.

CITIZENSHIP IDEALS

Citizenship isn't just about voting once every few years. Democracy works best when citizens get involved in government. There are several ways citizens can participate. They can send letters to their lawmakers or speak out about something important to them.

Was that an avalanche?

No. It's the voice of America's citizens.

Thank you, Super Citizen!

Just doing my job, ma'am.

Ideally, citizens work hard at being good people. They consider the needs of others in their community and country. They have the courage to confront wrongdoing.

VOTER TURNOUT AND CITIZENSHIP

Voter turnout has been declining for decades, but some studies suggest it's not the only measure of citizenship. Sometimes those who rarely vote continue to serve their communities and country as volunteers or as group organizers.

It's usually up to citizens to spur change. Before women were allowed to vote, both men and women organized, protested, and marched. Finally, in 1920, the 19th Amendment to the Constitution gave women the right to vote.

In the 1960s, African Americans were fed up with being denied jobs and education because of the color of their skin. Civil rights leader Dr. Martin Luther King Jr. urged his supporters to stage marches, sit-ins, and speeches. In 1964, their efforts paid off with the passage of the Civil Rights Act. This act guaranteed them the same rights as whites.

civil rights — the rights that all people have to freedom and equal treatment under the law

So how can you, as a citizen, make your community and country a better place? Don't wait until you are 18 and can vote.

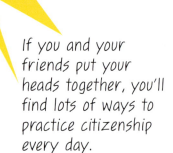

If you and your friends put your heads together, you'll find lots of ways to practice citizenship every day.

Thank you. This can of soup will help a family in need.

When you collect canned goods for a food drive, you're being a good citizen. If you attend a rally to protect the environment, you're being a citizen. Even speaking out at a city council or school board meeting is good citizenship.

I'm always happy to be a good citizen.

Citizens have the power to shape their neighborhoods, cities, and country. Whether at the voting booth or on an Internet blog, citizens have many ways to flex their democratic muscles.

HEALTH CARE   EDUCATION   ENVIRONMENT

Grrr. I'll get this issue into shape if it kills me.

President Abraham Lincoln summed up the role of U.S. citizens best. In his famous Gettysburg Address he said the U.S. government is a . . .

. . . government of the people, by the people, for the people . . .

Lincoln sure has a way with words.

He makes me want to be a better citizen.

TIME LINE

800–700 B.C. — The earliest citizenships emerge in Greek city-states.

800–700 BC

1886 — The Statue of Liberty is completed. It is a symbol of freedom and opportunity for millions of immigrants coming to America.

1886

1920 — The 19th Amendment to the U.S. Constitution grants women the right to vote.

VOTE!

1920

1964 — The Civil Rights Act bans discrimination in public places. It also guarantees access to public schools for all and outlaws employment discrimination.

CRA

EQUAL RIGHTS

1964

1791 — The 1st Amendment to the U.S. Constitution guarantees citizens the freedom of speech, press, religion, and assembly.

1791

1865 — The 13th Amendment to the U.S. Constitution outlaws slavery.

1865

1870 — The 15th Amendment to the U.S. Constitution grants the right to vote to former male slaves.

1870

2000 — Congress passes the Child Citizenship Act. Any child under the age of 18 who is adopted by a U.S. citizen and immigrates to the United States becomes an immediate citizen.

1971 — The 26th Amendment to the U.S. Constitution lowers the voting age for all citizens to 18 years of age.

1971

2000

GLOSSARY

amendment (uh-MEND-muhnt) — a change made to a law or a legal document

Bill of Rights (BIL UHV RITES) — a list of 10 amendments to the Constitution that protect your right to speak freely, to practice religion, and other important rights

civil rights (SIV-il RITES) — the rights that all people have to freedom and equal treatment under the law

constitution (kon-stuh-TOO-shuhn) — the system of laws that state the rights of the people and the powers of the government

deportation (di-por-TAY-shuhn) — the act of sending illegal immigrants back to their own country

Founding Father (FOUN-ding FAH-thur) — one of a handful of men who were important in helping the colonies become one country

illegal immigrant (i-LEE-guhl IM-uh-gruhnt) — a foreign-born person living in a country without legal permission

jury (JU-ree) — a group of people at a trial that decides whether the person accused of a crime is innocent or guilty

naturalization (nach-ur-uh-lye-ZAY-shuhn) — the process of giving citizenship to someone who was born in another country

political party (puh-LIT-uh-kuhl PAR-tee) — a group of people who share the same beliefs about how the government should operate

territory (TERR-uh-tor-ee) — land under control of a country

visa (VEE-zuh) — a document giving a person permission to enter a foreign country

READ MORE

Beier, Anne. *The Importance of Being an Active Citizen.* A Primary Source Library of American Citizenship. New York: Rosen, 2004.

Brown, Liz. *Civics.* Social Studies Essential Skills. New York: Weigl, 2008.

Burgan, Michael. *The Creation of the U.S. Constitution.* Graphic History. Mankato, Minn.: Capstone Press, 2007.

Hamilton, John. *Becoming a Citizen.* Government in Action! Edina, Minn.: ABDO, 2005.

O'Donnell, Liam. *Democracy.* Cartoon Nation. Mankato, Minn.: Capstone Press, 2008.

INTERNET SITES

FactHound offers a safe, fun way to find Internet sites related to this book. All of the sites on FactHound have been researched by our staff.

Here's how:
1. Visit www.facthound.com
2. Choose your grade level.
3. Type in this book ID 1429613319 for age-appropriate sites. You may also browse subjects by clicking on letters, or by clicking on pictures and words.
4. Click on the Fetch It button.

FactHound will fetch the best sites for you!

INDEX